PHOTO CREDITS

p. 11 - THE GRANGER COLLECTION, New York
p. 27 - Colorado Historical Society
p. 29 - The Plumas County Museum, Quincy, CA
p. 32 - The Bettmann Archive, New York, NY: UPI/Bettmann Newsphotos, New York, NY
p. 33 - Neg. No. 2A9604, Courtesy Department Library Services,
        American Museum of Natural History
p. 37 - The Bettman Archive, New York, NY,
        National Archives and Records Administration,
        Washington, DC, Record Group 401
p. 39 - Private Collection
p. 41 - National Aeronautics and Space Administration (NASA)
p. 45 - National Aeronautics and Space Administration (NASA)
p. 47 - National Aeronautics and Space Administration (NASA)

Text copyright © 1995 by Wade Hudson.
Illustrations copyright © 1995 by Ron Garnett.
All rights reserved. Published by Scholastic Inc.
Printed in the U.S.A.
ISBN 0-590-06677-3
HELLO READER!, CARTWHEEL BOOKS, and the CARTWHEEL BOOKS logo are registered
trademarks of Scholastic Inc.

15 14 13 12 11   23   03 02 01 00

Produced by
Just Us Books
301 Main Street
Orange, NJ 07050

GREAT BLACK HEROES

FIVE BRAVE EXPLORERS

by Wade Hudson
Illustrated by Ron Garnett

Hello Reader!

Scholastic Inc.

New York Toronto London Auckland Sydney

Produced by Just Us Books, Inc.

Esteban Dorantes

Early American Explorer
born circa 1500 — died circa 1539

It was February 1527. Five big ships waited at a seaport in Spain. Hundreds of people were on board. There were soldiers, settlers, and people looking for adventure. They were sailing to the new land called America. King Ferdinand was sending them there to explore the territory called Florida.

Would they find riches—gold and silver? Would they find danger? No one knew.

One of the people on board was a

young man named Esteban Dorantes. Esteban was born in Morocco, in North Africa. One day he was captured and brought to Spain to be a slave. Andres Dorantes was his master. Esteban was traveling with Dorantes to the new land.

In April 1528, the expedition reached Florida. Three hundred of the strongest men were chosen to go inland. Esteban was one of those selected. The rest of the people, including women and children, remained on the ships.

The three hundred men met unfriendly Native Americans inland. The men fought battles with the Native Americans. They attacked Native American villages. The warriors of the village called Apalachen were strong and brave. They fought back with bows and arrows and the Spaniards ran. Many of the Spaniards were killed. Those who survived tried to return to the ships.

Esteban and the other survivors traveled

through swamps filled with dangerous animals. The men suffered from the extremely hot, humid weather. Swarms of mosquitoes that carried diseases attacked them. Every day men died from diseases, fever, and starvation. The ships were nowhere in sight.

Then the men decided to travel by water. They built five wooden boats and set sail. But they sailed in the wrong direction. They passed land that would become the states of Georgia, Alabama, Mississippi, and Louisiana. Three boats were lost at sea. The other two boats crashed off the coast of Texas. Esteban was in one of the boats. His master, Dorantes, was in another. Both survived the crash.

Esteban and his remaining companions were captured by a Native American tribe called the Capoques. For nearly five years, the explorers lived as prisoners of the Native Americans. By now only four explorers were left—Andres Dorantes, Alfonso del Castillo Maldonaldo, Cabeza de Vaca, and Esteban.

Esteban was a smart prisoner. He became friendly with his captors. He learned their language, and he learned about the land. In 1534, Esteban, Dorantes, de Vaca, and Maldonaldo escaped. They decided to go to the Spanish settlement in Mexico City. Esteban led the way through the wilderness. He had watched the ways of the Native Americans, so he knew how to find food and how to keep safe from wild animals. He kept his companions alive.

Esteban made friends quickly with Native Americans along the way. He learned their languages easily. Altogether, he knew at least six Native American languages.

Months passed. One year passed. Then two. But Esteban did not give up hope of finding Mexico City.

A diagram of Mexico City during the 1500s

Finally, the men reached Mexico City in 1536. They were escorted by Spanish soldiers they had met on their journey.

The four men told the people of Mexico City of their great adventure. Very few white or black men had explored such a wide area of the new land before. Esteban and his companions had traveled three thousand miles.

The people of Mexico City treated the explorers like heroes. Esteban enjoyed the excitement. But there was one question on his mind. During the journey, he and his companions were equals. But what would happen to him now? he wondered. Would he be treated as a free man? Or would he be treated as a slave again? Soon he got his answer.

Esteban had saved Dorantes' life many times. Esteban had great courage and wisdom. He had led the difficult trip across the country. But Dorantes still considered this brave explorer a slave. He sold Esteban to the governor of Mexico City.

Esteban's days as an explorer were not over, though. He was asked to guide an expedition to find the "Seven Cities of Gold." On this trip, he explored land that is now

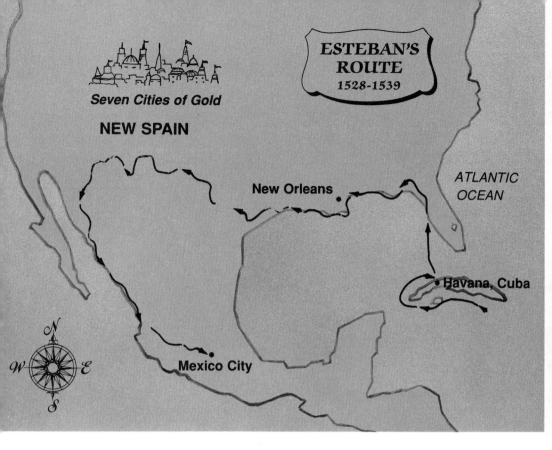

Esteban traveled across the southern part of the United States into Mexico.

Arizona and New Mexico.

Sadly, Esteban was killed during the expedition. But he had made his important contributions to history. Esteban was one of the first blacks to explore America. His legend still lives among Native American folklore in the Southwest.

Jean Baptiste Pointe DuSable

Founder of Chicago
born circa 1745 — died 1818

The "quiet, black Frenchman": That's what the Native Americans of the Midwest called Jean Baptiste Pointe DuSable.

DuSable was born around 1745 in Haiti. His father was a white, French sea captain, and his mother had been a black slave. After his mother died, DuSable's father took him to France to go to school. DuSable became well educated. He learned to speak English, French, and Spanish.

Later, DuSable returned to Haiti and worked as a seaman on his father's boats. When he was twenty years old, he and his close friend, Jacques Clemorgan, sailed for America. Their boat wrecked near New Orleans, Louisiana, during a storm. Luckily, the two friends were not hurt. They made their way to New Orleans. But that was not good.

In New Orleans, black men and women were sold into slavery. People thought any black person walking about the streets without a white person was a runaway slave. DuSable and Clemorgan were afraid of being captured and sold into slavery. They left New Orleans as quickly as they could.

They traveled by boat up the Mississippi River. And as they made their way north, they trapped animals and sold the furs. They soon settled in St. Louis, Missouri, and became successful fur traders.

After a while, DuSable moved to Fort

Peoria, Illinois, and continued his fur trading business. He met a woman named Kittihawa. Kittihawa was a Native American. She was a member of the Potowatomi clan. DuSable married Kittihawa in a Native American ceremony. He even became a member of her clan.

DuSable and Clemorgan sold fur.

DuSable often traveled to Canada to trap animals. Then he would return to Illinois to sell the furs. On every trip, he would rest at a place that the Native Americans called Eschikago. Many traders stopped there.

In 1779, DuSable had an idea. He would build a trading post in Eschikago. He would buy furs from trappers and sell them supplies they needed.

Two years later, DuSable, his wife, son,

and members of the Potowatomi clan went to
Eschikago. They built houses, barns, and
smokehouses to store meat. DuSable's house
had five rooms and a fireplace. It served as
his trading post. Other buildings were added.
Soon, Eschikago was a growing settlement.

DuSable's daughter Suzzanne was the
first child born there. She was named for his
mother.

Many traders and settlers stopped at

Eschikago. It was the best trading post between St. Louis and Montreal, Canada.

In 1800, DuSable sold the settlement and his business to Jean Lalime for twelve thousand dollars. John Kinzie was a witness to the deal. Kinzie also carried the proof-of-sale certificate to St. Joseph, Michigan, to be registered. He registered the sale in his own name.

DuSable and his family moved back to Peoria, Illinois. DuSable owned eight hundred acres of land there. Kittihawa died nine years later, and DuSable moved to St. Charles, Missouri. He died there in 1818.

The settlement Jean Baptiste Pointe DuSable started is now the city of Chicago. It is one of the largest cities in the world. The world's tallest building, the Sears Tower, is located there. It also has one of the world's busiest airports.

For over 150 years, DuSable was not recognized for his important contribution to this city. Instead, John Kinzie was called the founder of Chicago. Finally, in 1968, the great explorer was officially named the founder of the city of Chicago.

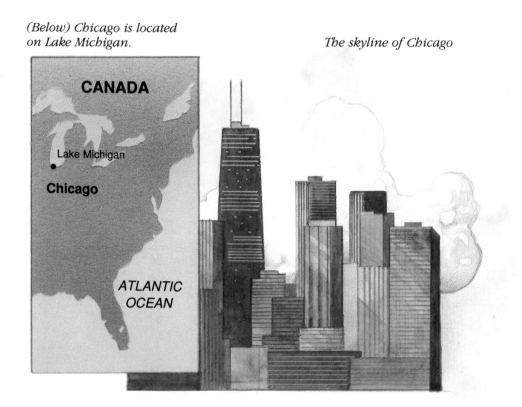

(Below) Chicago is located on Lake Michigan.

The skyline of Chicago

James Pierce Beckwourth

American Trailblazer
born 1798 — died 1866

James Beckwourth climbed the Sierra Nevada Mountains ahead of the twelve men in his party. He was in a big hurry.

The men had come to the Sierra Nevada Mountains looking for gold. Beckwourth, however, had something else on his mind. He was looking for an opening through the mountains so that people would not have to climb the mountains to get to the other side.

(Left) James Beckwourth helps a fallen friend.

The mountain range spreads four hundred miles in eastern California. Crossing it was very difficult.

Beckwourth found the opening he was looking for. It was the most wonderful sight he had ever seen. There was a beautiful, green valley with many different flowers growing everywhere. There were magnificent birds, and all kinds of wild animals. Right away Beckwourth knew he had discovered something very special. He had found a path across the Sierra Nevada Mountains to the

Long Valley in California. It was a much shorter route than any other one.

In the years that followed, it was named "Beckwourth's Pass." Thousands of settlers and gold seekers used this route to get to California. Beckwourth led the first wagon train through his discovery. Later, the Western Pacific Railroad also used it.

For several years, Beckwourth lived in the valley near the pass. He ran a hotel and trading post there. But he soon grew restless to travel. He was an adventurer at heart.

James Pierce Beckwourth was born in Frederick County, Virginia, in 1798. His father was a white slave owner and his mother was a black slave. When he was seven or eight, his father moved the family to St. Louis, Missouri.

When young James reached the age of fourteen, his father sent him to live and work with a white blacksmith named George Caster. At first, James did not want to be a blacksmith. But he grew to like it.

When James was nineteen, he fell in love with a young slave girl. He would stay out late at night visiting his friend. Caster didn't like that. Caster had strict rules James had to obey. The two men did not always agree.

One day, James and the blacksmith got into a fight. James hit the blacksmith and fled. He never returned home.

James worked in a salt mine for a while. He traveled to New Orleans, and then back to St. Louis. One day a man named General William Henry Ashley and a group of men were heading west to trap animals. The animals' furs would be worth a lot of money in the east. Beckwourth joined the group. And this was the start of Beckwourth's life as one of this country's greatest frontiersmen.

James P. Beckwourth

During his lifetime, he traveled to New Mexico, Arizona, Florida, and Mexico. For six years, he lived in Montana with Native American people called the Crow. He even became their chief. This daring frontiersman survived many battles and adventures with them. He finally left them and went off looking for new adventures.

Beckwourth died in 1866. The Army had sent Beckwourth to make peace with the Crow. Legend has it that many of the Crow remembered Beckwourth as their chief from years before. They asked him to be their chief again and he refused. So he was poisoned to keep him from leaving again. But that story was not proven.

Many black explorers and frontiersmen helped to open the West. James Pierce Beckwourth was one of the greatest.

(Left) A map showing
Beckwourth's Pass

OREGON

CALIFORNIA

NEVADA

Pit River

Pyramid Lake

Beckwourth's Pass

Feather
River

Truckee River

CALIFORNIA
TRAIL

Lake Tahoe

American River

SACRAMENTO

Beckwourth's stirrup and bullet mold

Beckwourth's cabin located
near the path he discovered

A wooden table
Beckwourth is
said to have made

29

Matthew A. Henson

North Pole Explorer
born 1866 — died 1955

The most northern part of the earth has below-freezing temperatures. Ice covers the area. This is the North Pole.

In 1893, no one had been to the North Pole. That year Admiral Robert E. Peary and Matthew Henson set out to reach the North Pole. But they were unsuccessful. They tried again in 1898, but failed. In 1909, they set out once more.

Peary, Henson, and a group that included explorer Robert Bartlett took off for the Pole. They sailed on a long voyage from New York City to Canada. Next, they set up a base camp at Camp Columbia, Canada. The camp was about 450 miles from the North Pole. In March 1909, the group packed dog sleds with food and supplies. Then they

Matthew Henson

Admiral Robert E. Peary

The Roosevelt took Henson and his party from New York City to Ellesmere Island near the North Pole.

headed over the polar sea ice toward the North Pole.

Some of the men suffered from the harsh cold weather. They had to return to the camp. Finally, Peary selected Henson and four Inuit guides—Ootah, Seegloo, Egingwah, and Ooqueah—to make the last leg of the journey. It was early April 1909. They were closer than ever to really reaching the North Pole.

Henson, Peary, and their guides traveled over the ice and snow. Peary's feet were injured. He could not walk as quickly as Henson. So Henson and his guides walked ahead—and disaster struck.

Along the way, Matthew Henson stepped out on a large cake of ice. *CRACK!* The ice gave way. Henson fell into the icy water below. The water temperature was bitter cold: −15 degrees Fahrenheit. In only a few minutes, Matthew Henson would have frozen to death.

Suddenly, there was a tug on Henson's hood. Someone was pulling him from the water. It was Ootah. Quickly, Ootah helped Henson pull off his wet boots and clothes and put on dry ones. Ootah shook the water from the furs Henson wore before the water turned to ice. Then Henson, Ootah, and Seegloo moved on. Admiral Robert E. Peary, Egingwah, and Ooqueah followed. The North Pole was less than thirty-five miles away.

Henson got closer and closer to the

Pole. Finally, he stopped. He looked around. Had he reached the North Pole? Henson set up camp there and waited for Peary.

When the Admiral arrived, he made observations from different points. He returned to the camp and made an announcement. The camp was at the exact point of the North Pole. He had Henson and the four guides stand on a ridge and he photographed them. Henson held the American flag. He felt proud. It had been an exciting adventure.

•

Matthew Henson was born in Charles County, Maryland, in 1866. After his mother died, he lived with an uncle in Washington, D.C. Henson always liked adventure. When he was fourteen years old, he signed on as a cabin boy on a ship called the *Katie Hines*. He was a member of the crew for five years.

Henson met Peary in 1887, when Henson was working in a clothing store in

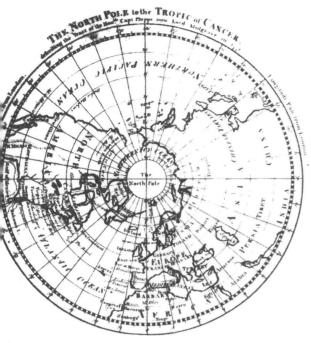

An early chart of the North Pole

The explorer poses with his sled and dogs.

Henson taking time to relax

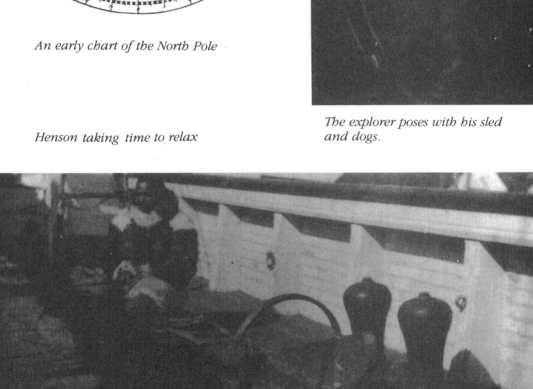

Washington, D.C. Peary liked Henson right away. Peary offered Henson a job as his personal servant. Henson didn't want to be a servant. But he was interested in a trip Peary had planned to Nicaragua, South America. It was a chance for him to travel again. For more than twenty years, the two men took many trips together.

●

On April 7, 1909, the great explorers began their journey back from the North Pole. They were very happy about their victory.

Robert E. Peary became famous. Peary was awarded a gold medal by the National Geographic Society. Robert Bartlett was also awarded a medal although he didn't even make the final trip to the North Pole. Matthew Henson was ignored.

For many years, the white world did not recognize Henson's great achievement. The black community, however, presented him with a number of awards. Finally, on January

28, 1944, Congress authorized a medal for all the men on the North Pole expedition. A year later, Henson was presented with a silver medal for outstanding service to the United States Government.

This great explorer died in 1955. On April 6, 1988, his remains were reburied with full military honors at Arlington National Cemetery. It was a most suitable honor for a great black American.

The state of Maryland honored this great explorer with this plaque.

Mae C. Jemison

Space Explorer
born 1956 —

At the Kennedy Space Center in Florida, scientists got ready for an exciting launch. The space shuttle *Endeavour* was on the launch pad. Its nose pointed straight up toward the clouds. Inside, seven astronauts sat very still in their seats. Each waited for *Endeavour* to blast off into space. One of the astronauts was Mae C. Jemison.

When Mae was in grade school, she dreamed about being an astronaut and traveling through space. On September 12, 1992, her dream was about to come true.

The countdown began. "10. 9. 8. . ."

Many things could go wrong. The launch could be delayed. "7. 6. 5. 4. . ."

Once, a spaceship exploded just after it took off. All of the astronauts aboard were killed.

"3. 2. 1. Liftoff!"

Endeavour began to rise. Then, it soared above the clouds. The people at the space center cheered. The launch was a success. Mae Jemison's voyage had begun.

•

Mae was born in Decatur, Georgia. Her family moved to Chicago when she was very young. Her parents told her to study hard and learn as much as she could. Mae loved to learn. She spent many hours in the library reading books about science and science fiction.

Mae grew up in the 1960s. The whole

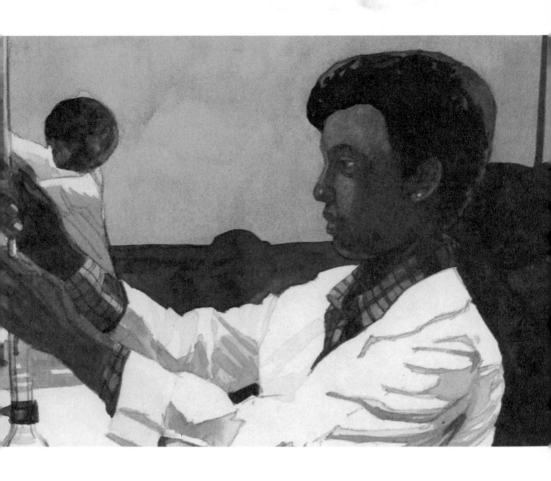

country was excited about space travel and space exploration. Like many other girls and boys, Mae wanted to be an astronaut. But there were no women astronauts in America then. There were no black astronauts, either. So what were *her* chances? Mae just kept on dreaming about exploring in space. Nothing was going to stop her.

When she was sixteen, Mae graduated from high school. Her grades were very good. Stanford University gave her a scholarship and she went there. Mae wanted to be a doctor, so she went to medical school. Later Mae joined the Peace Corps to help needy people in other countries. She went to Sierra Leone and Liberia in West Africa. She used what she had learned in medical school to help the people there.

But Mae still dreamed of becoming an astronaut. She returned to the United States in 1985. She applied to the astronaut program at the National Aeronautics and Space Administration (NASA). Mae waited for a reply. Then the spaceship *Challenger* exploded while on its way into space. All seven astronauts were killed. NASA stopped taking new astronauts.

But Mae was not scared. She applied again when the astronaut program began once more.

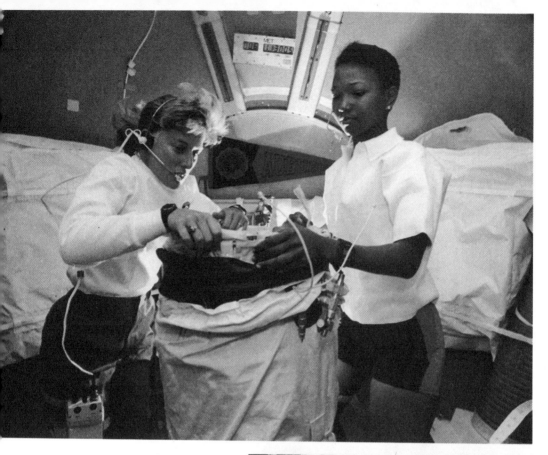

(Above) Astronaut Jemison and fellow astronaut N. Jan Davis in training aboard Endeavour

(Right) Dr. Jemison doing scientific research

In the meantime, she was working for CIGNA Health Plans of California and attending graduate engineering classes in Los Angeles. One day, in August 1987, a man from NASA called Jemison with great news. Jemison had been chosen for the astronaut program. She was very happy. Nearly two thousand people had applied to the program. Only fifteen had been selected. Mae Jemison felt really special.

The training program was hard. Astronauts must be strong and fit, so they exercise. They study mathematics, earth resources, meteorology, guidance and navigation, astronomy, physics, and computers. There is much to learn to get ready for space travel.

After training for a year, Mae C. Jemison was officially an astronaut. She was eager to travel into space, but she had to wait her turn. Finally, in 1991, she was selected for the space flight on the *Endeavour.*

(Left) Dr. Jemison, a physician, wears monitoring gear during test aboard Endeavour.

(Below) Dr. Jemison conducts test in zero-gravity during space mission.

Now Mae had to train for the trip. She was chosen to be the science mission specialist. She had experiments to do while in space.

The day finally arrived. As *Endeavour* sped away from Earth, Mae C. Jemison became the first black woman to explore space.

It was a great day for this proud American. She was very happy. Her dream had come true.